A DORSET CAMERA

1914~1945

David Burnett

The Dovecote Press

Text © David Burnett 1975

First published by The Dovecote Press
Stanbridge, Wimborne, Dorset

Fifth reprint 1985

ISBN 0 9503518 1 4

The text is set in Linotype Pilgrim
and printed and bound in Great Britain by
Biddles Ltd, Guildford and King's Lynn

Contents

Introduction

The first photographs in this book were taken sixty-one years ago in 1914. A person born in that year would neither recognise the world of their infancy nor yet be eligible for an old-age pension. Such are the contradictions of the 20th century. So much has happened in so few years that already the memories of childhood have become the stuff of history.

In 1914 the horse was still the undisputed master of the highway. Dorset's 1,200 motoring pioneers travelled a countryside that boasted neither petrol station nor tarmac road. The speed limit was 20 m.p.h, and there it would remain until 1930 when, for four glorious years, anybody over seventeen could drive at any speed they liked without ever having to pass a test. In 1914 there were no tractors or wireless sets, no refrigerators, few aeroplanes, and no mains electricity. Houses were lit by paraffin lamps, and towns by gas. Most of the county's quarter of a million population lived, worked, and died in the same village as their forefathers. The school-leaving age stood at twelve; the agricultural labourer's weekly wage at 12s. 6d. Only in Poole, and to a lesser extent Dorchester, Weymouth, and Swanage, where the lines of red-brick villas had begun their march out into the countryside, could one sense what the future had in store. The customs, traditions, and sense of continuity of the Victorian Age were self-evident. It was as if Dorset, like all other rural counties, had entered the 20th century without ever leaving the 19th.

The photographs in this book span 31 years. Of these, eleven were spent in fighting two World Wars. If the First ended a way of life that seemingly had existed since time immemorial, the Second has shaped the world we live in today. During the years of peace that separate 1918 from 1939, a period of extraordinary progress and invention – balanced by unemployment, the General Strike, and Depression – revolutionised rural England. Anyone doubting the extent of that change need only contrast the cavalry squadron of Dorset Yeomanry in 1915 (plate 20) with the self-confident American G.I.s packed into their landing craft before D-Day (plate 128).

With progress came not only the "flapper" and "rag-time" but also tarmac roads, telephone kiosks, and a national electricity grid. Just as the evacuation of 1940 was to introduce the Cockney barrow-boy to the "Do'set" hurdle-maker's son, so too did the 'twenties taste for hiking and seaside holidays, for driving the Austin Seven or Bullnose Morris up Bulbarrow, for taking the charabanc on a day's outing to West Bay, assist in the breakdown of suspicion between the countryman and city dweller. By 1939 all England was a potential suburb, and Dorset, along with its own special character and traditions, had been dragged, bootlaces first, into the 20th century.

During these years the Forestry Commission was set up, and the first council houses built. Health, Pension, and Insurance Acts were passed that laid the foundations for a welfare state. By 1930 nine out of ten homes had a wireless. The "talkies" were sufficiently popular to give each of Dorset's market-towns its own cinema. Movements such as the Women's Institute and Young Farmers Club encouraged people to meet, to discuss common interests and problems. Lending libraries, new schools and hospitals, all played their part. West Dorset was severely hit by the agricultural Depression, and the founding of both acreage subsidies for barley and oats and marketing boards for milk and bacon helped in the gradual return to prosperity.

Dorset's character made itself felt beyond its own boundaries with the aid of four special factors – of whom the first was Thomas Hardy. His novels of Wessex had made the Dorset countryside internationally known, and this encouraged positive efforts to preserve its coombes and downland, wild-life and coast. Weymouth's position as a seaside resort was also important. On Bank Holiday weekend in 1939 the G.W.R. brought 55,000 visitors to the town, and with the holidaymakers came the seeds of a new industry – that of tourism. The opening of the T.U.C. Memorial Cottages in Tolpuddle in 1934, and the four seasons of excavation at Maiden Castle between 1934 and 1937, also focused national attention on Dorset. If one was proof of a century of social improvement, the other reminded the country of the wealth and diversity of its heritage.

The final photograph in this book was taken just after the war in Europe had ended in May 1945. The Home Guard was already on Stand Down, but barbed wire and gun emplacements still shrouded the Dorset beaches. Weymouth and Sherborne were still scarred by bomb-sites, and rationing was still in force. But the gas-masks could go into the attic; "Windy Ridge", a Dorchester air-raid shelter, could be safely abandoned; and the front garden once again sown with grass seed instead of potatoes. The evidence of five long years of war were everywhere; but from all over the world Dorset folk were returning home in demob suits to the uncertainties of peace.

That was thirty years ago. To some it seems like yesterday: to others a century away. There will be many who will recognise people and places in this book. Some who will come face to face with themselves. I have tried to be totally accurate about information and dates, but in some cases it is impossible to guarantee their accuracy. Either no one can remember, or everyone: and if it is the latter, conflicting stories abound. For every memory there is a different ending, and this uncertainty about quite recent events explains how easily facts become hazy, the present the past.

The small "Box" camera made possible many of the photographs in this book. It also affected their quality and quantity. Already photographs of the period are rarer than those of the 19th century. The popular snapshots of the 'twenties and 'thirties were taken with less care, and were more often lost, than those contained in the embossed albums of the Victorian professional or well-to-do amateur.

We tend to take the inventions of the 20th century for granted; to ignore the immediate past, and regret instead that the tides of change have washed over the patterns of pre-1914 England. But in 1929 there were still 13,000 cart-horses in Dorset, in 1969 perhaps 50. The lanes are as leafy today as they were in 1930. It is just that there are less of them, and proportionally more people, main roads, and houses. The pattern is kaleidoscopic, always changing. Moving so slowly that we rarely seem to notice the turning of the clock, moving so fast that we never have time to sit down and remember.

August 1975   D.B.

Acknowledgements

I am most grateful to the following for allowing me to include their photographs in this book: Dorset County Museum, Dorchester: photograph numbers, 2, 4, 6, 7, 8, 9, 12, 16, 19, 31, 36, 37, 38, 42, 45, 46, 50, 58, 59, 64, 65, 67, 69, 70, 71, 74, 77, 78, 79, 82, 83, 84, 85, 90, 92, 96, 97, 98, 99, 101, 102, 103, 104, 105, 114, 115. The Brewery Farm Museum: 66. The Bridport Museum and Art Gallery: 26, 29, 44, 81, 109. L. W. Chisman: 5, 24. A. T. P. Cooper: 126. The County Records Office, Dorchester: 122. Mrs. Cox: 40, 107. Mrs. P. Dimond: 34, 89. The Cecil Durston Collection of Portland Photographs: 23, 73. Mrs. J. Evans: 13, 54, 56. The Gillingham Museum of Local History: 39. A. G. Greening: 55. The Guildhall Museum, Poole: 25, 60. Miss M. Harris: 48, 116. A. Hawkes: 43, 80. D. Hindley: 68, 86. The Imperial War Museum: 14, 111, 112, 123, 125, 132, 133. H. V. F. Johnstone: 18. S. C. King: 28. Mrs. E. M. Lamb: 3, 57, 134. Mrs. I. M. Moore: 88. Mrs. J. Nash: 47, 61. J. Oldfield: 15. P. E. Payne: 49. The Gerald Pitman Sherborne Pictorial Record Collection: 41, 108. Poole Pottery: 72. The Priest's House Museum, Wimborne: 62, 63, 127. The Raymond Rogers Collection of Sturminster Newton Photographs: 1, 30, 33, 53, 87, 91, 94, 120. The Sherborne Museum: 22, 32, 35, 93. Sherborne Town Council: 124. F. G. Short: 20. F. Staff: 11, 27. The Wareham Pictorial Museum: 21, 100. Mrs. D. Wareham: 95. J. Wells: 110. Weymouth Public Library: 10, 17, 51, 52, 75, 76, 106, 113, 117, 118, 119, 121, 128, 129, 130, 131, 135.

I am grateful to the following for permission to make quotations in the text: Jonathan Cape Ltd. for an extract from the *Selected Letters of T. E. Lawrence*, and the Cambridge University Press for an extract from Eric Benfield's *Purbeck Shop*.

Although it has proved impossible to use all the many hundreds of photographs that were sent to me in response to a letter I had published in the Dorset press, I am very grateful to all those who took the time and trouble to write to me enclosing photographs, many of them precious and irreplaceable.

Once again I am indebted to Roger Peers, Curator of the Dorset County Museum, for his encouragement and invaluable assistance. I am also grateful to the following for their friendly help with the research: 'Skylark' Durston, Gerald Pitman, Ray Rogers, John Sales (Bridport Museum), Graham Smith (The Guildhall Museum, Poole), John Woodhouse (Hall & Woodhouse Ltd.), Miss H. M. Coles (The Priest's House Museum), Miss M. Holmes (The County Records Office), Mr. Turner (Weymouth Public Library), Robert Fookes (The Brewery Farm Museum), K. Allen (Wareham Pictorial Museum), Les Hayward (Poole Pottery), W. W. Slade (Gillingham Museum), M. Brennan (The Imperial War Museum), John Oldfield, Mrs. Judy Evans, Harry Johnstone, Allan Cooper, S. S. Rose (Sherborne Town Council), Miss D. M. Rogers (Sherborne Museum), Mr. L. LeBreton (Assistant Controller of Licences, Dorset County Council), and the staff of the Dorset County Museum.

Goodbye to All That ~ Dorset in 1914

2. (*Overleaf*) Weymouth beach during the idyllic summer of 1914. War lay one month away, but in the same week as this photograph was taken Austria-Hungary declared war on Serbia, and the 1st Fleet left Portland for battle stations. For the holidaymaker the town had never been so popular. Cinema goers had a choice between "Two Little Nibs" and "Antony & Cleopatra". The "Follies" Revue was on at the Pavilion (tickets 2d. to 2s. 6d.); and at the "Arcadia" the World Welterweight Champion, "The Dixie Kid", was waiting to take on all comers for a £40 purse – then a year's wage for a farm labourer.

3. A wedding group at Portesham in 1914, after the marriage between Edward Thorne, the village blacksmith, and Lucy Hodder.

4. The sheep struck dead by lightning at William Hunt's Thorncombe farm near Blandford in June 1914. The *County Chronicle* reported that a shepherd's crook was standing by and "thus attracted the current to the crowd of affrighted sheep huddled near."

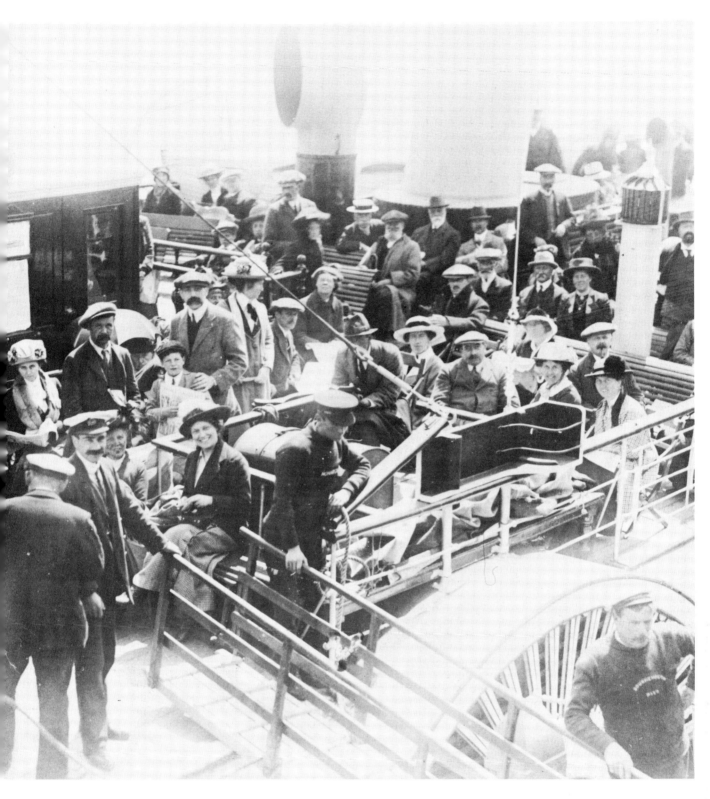

Boarding the "Monarch" at Poole in May 1914. The 315-ton paddle steamer was built by Cosens
& Co. in 1888 and broken up in 1952 when she was costing £3,000 a year to keep up to Board of
Trade regulations. Berthed between the wars at Poole, she had a cross-channel certificate and
was used on both the Cherbourg and Alderney runs. The "Monarch" was one of many steamers
chartered to accompany the ill-fated "Titanic" at the start of her maiden voyage.

6. The salon of Kingston Maurward House, Stinsford, the home of the Balfours in 1914.

8 The "Victoria" leaving Lulworth Cove before going on to Swanage, Studland, and Poole in the summer of 1914. Before and between the wars the coastal paddle steamer calling in at Dorset's steeply shelving shingle beaches was amongst its most popular pleasures and sights.

7. The front parlour of a tenanted cottage lived in by the Wills family at Turnworth in about 1914. Note the hams and flitches of bacon hanging to the right of the fireplace. Both photographs capture the essence of a vanished Dorset. If the cottager's family pig was to depart in a sea of red-tape and health regulations, the country-house way of life was gradually undermined in the post-war years by rising wages, taxation, and the shortage of domestic staff.

9. Major Radclyffe's sturgeon aboard the roof of his 35-hp Daimler in 1914. The sturgeon – renowned for caviare – was caught at Hyde Mill on the River Piddle. Dorset County Museum contains a 203-lb. stuffed sturgeon caught on the Frome near Bindon Mill in 1911.

10. (*Overleaf*) The scene on Weymouth Esplanade in May 1914 on the presentation of the town's Freedom to Admiral Lord Charles Beresford, the retired C.-in-C. of the Channel Fleet. At a celebratory dinner Admiral Beresford proudly announced that as a midshipman he had often amused himself by firing rockets at convicts building Portland breakwater.

11. Albert Holborrow aboard his home-made 14-foot boat before leaving West Bay, Bridport, in July 1914, in an attempt to sail the Atlantic. Although he had stores for three months Holborrow, both elderly and a cripple, had never been to sea before, and he was found a week later adrift off Plymouth thinking he had left England well astern. "The plucky voyager was strongly advised against undertaking so foolhardy a voyage", and towed into harbour. Holborrow complained that although his boat had a "natty white appearance" it lacked speed, but he insisted that he had attempted the voyage for his health rather than as a wager or for "'the glory of the thing".

12. An impressive display of British Naval strength anchored off Branksome Chine in either 1913 or 1914. In July 1914 60 ships of four Cruiser Battle Squadrons gathered in Portland before going directly to battle stations. The *Dorset County Chronicle* of the period records a certain amount of inebriation amongst the 7,000 ratings of the Fleet as they enjoyed their shore-leave in Weymouth's many pubs.

The Great War

EY10

13. *(Overleaf)* Jack Biss of Thornford in 1914. Jack Biss enlisted in the Dorset Yeomanry when he was under age and was killed on 26 February 1916, during the Agagia Charge, when he had just turned eighteen. The charge of the Dorset Yeomanry during the Mesopotamian campaign was amongst the final and most famous cavalry charges of the war. 32 members of the Yeomanry were killed at the expense of some 300 Senussi tribesmen.

14. H.M.S. "Formidable" in 1914. The sinking of the 15,000-ton battleship by a torpedo in Lyme Bay just after midnight on 1 January 1915 was the first major naval disaster of the war. The "Formidable" had been built in 1901, had four 12-inch guns, and was part of the Atlantic Fleet. Out of a ship's complement of 750, only 199 were saved. Captain Loxley went down with his ship, but his dog lies buried in Abbotsbury churchyard.

15. The funeral of those who died on board a pinnace from the "Formidable", washed ashore on Lyme Regis Marine Parade during the gale that followed the battleship's sinking. Amongst those supposedly lying dead on the floor of the "Pilot Boat Inn" prior to the funeral was A.B. John Cowan. After being licked for half an hour by the landlord's rough-haired cross-bred collie "Lassie" it was realised that the seaman was breathing. This incident led to the creation of the legendary sheepdog "Lassie".

Swanage men who volunteered for Naval service during the
4-18 war photographed in 1920.

17. H.M.S. "Hood" being manoeuvred into position across the
southern entrance to Portland harbour in November 1914 before
being sunk as an anti-submarine obstacle. The "Hood" had been
built in 1891, removed from the fighting list in 1911 because of
her low freeboard and used as a torpedo target. Part of her hull
still remains in the harbour and is recommended as a place to
catch whiting.

18. A captured German submarine, "U 107", in Poole harbour in 1919.

19. Winston Churchill, then First Lord of the Admiralty, escorting George V from Blandford Station on his arrival by Royal Train to inspect the Royal Naval Division at the Camp on 25 February 1915. Amongst the officers in Hood Battalion of the 9,000-man Division were Rupert Brooke the poet, Bernard Freyberg, and Lieut. Asquith – the Prime Minister's son. Two days later, dressed in web equipment and pith helmets, the Division marched to Shillingstone and thence travelled by train and steamer to Gallipoli where it suffered 75 per cent casualties.

20. No. 2 Troop, "C" Squadron, the Dorset Yeomanry in front of Sherborne House, now Lord Digby's School, in early 1915. Four squadrons were raised at Sherborne, Gillingham, Blandford, and Dorchester, and after being used for coastal patrol became part of the 2nd Mounted Division and were landed at Suvla Bay during the Gallipoli campaign. Casualities were appalling. Out of 362 men and 15 officers only 66 were not killed or wounded in the 10 weeks the Yeomanry served in the Dardanelles.

21. The 17th Field Bakery at Worgret Camp, Wareham in 1915. The Camp had been started to house the volunteers for "Kitchener's Army". At first conditions were terrible, and the town's inhabitants were forced to help feed, clothe and look after the confused recruits. By 1915 the situation had improved. Wareham pubs were closed at 9 p.m. to avoid drunkenness, waggon-loads of beef, mutton, cheese, and jam were shipped in, and Field Bakeries set up. During the day, the recruits, "who are a smart lot, just the sort of fellows that the Germans will hardly care to face", spent their time drilling.

22. The Local Volunteer Defence Force posed outside the Armoury of Sherborne School in 1917. After training with wooden rifles and without uniforms the Force was organised into proper Battalions in 1916. The men were all either under or over age or unfit for active service, and the 17 detachments raised in Dorset spent much of the time digging trenches in case invasion should follow the German spring offensive of 1918.

23. Typical of photographs carried by soldiers in France during the Great War, this one belonged to Sapper Jimmy Durston of Portland, and shows his four children – Kathleen, Dorothy, Winnie, and "Skylark" – all of whom are still alive.

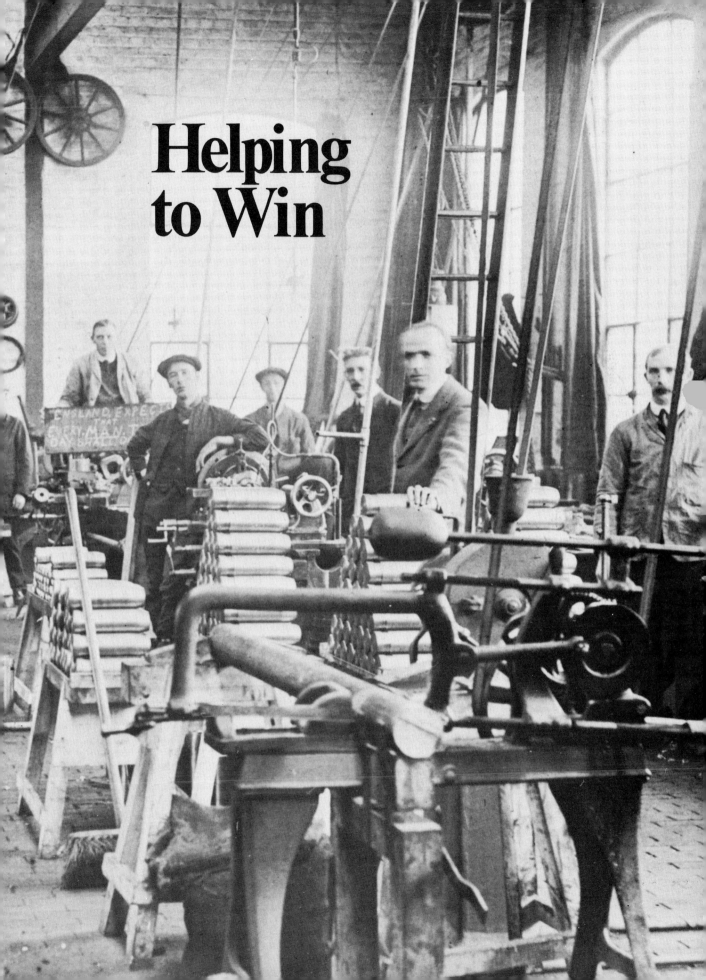

Helping
to Win

24. (*Overleaf*) Making shell cases in the fitters' shop of the Bournemouth Gas & Water Co. in 1915. The serious shortage of shells on the Western Front led to all engineering works being switched to war work early in the year. Nearly 300 men of the company served during the 1914-18 war, and during the Second World War in 1941 the Bourne Valley works were badly bombed.

25. Building coal bunkers for Bournemouth Gas & Water Co. on Poole Quay in 1917. By this stage of the war able-bodied men exempt from the Army were rare, and the company advertised widely for the work-force at a £3-a-week wage. When the gas section of the company was nationalised in 1949 it supplied a 700-square-mile area.

26. Bridport councillors in East St. at the end of "Business Men's Week", 1918. The National Committee asked the town to purchase £15,000-worth of War Bonds, sufficient for six aeroplanes, and Bridport responded by raising £69,070, enough for two squadrons.

27. Volunteers joining the Dorsetshire Regiment at Bridport in August 1914 in response to Kitchener's appeal for half a million volunteers. In six weeks 3,000 men joined the Regiment. By the time the war ended in November 1918 4,060 men had lost their lives serving with the Regiment.

28. Crowning the May Queen in the vicarage gardens at Motcombe in 1915

29. (*Overleaf*) The Army commandeering horses at the Artillery Parade Ground, Bridport, in August 1914. Farmers, tradesmen, and carriers were expected to accept the price offered by the Army Board vet, and many were left short-handed for harvesting and delivery work. Only two drays were left at the station for hauling goods.

31. An ambulance given by the Dorset Auto-mobile Club to the Wimborne Group of V.A.D. hospitals for use during the Great War. The Wimborne Group consisted of seven hospitals amongst them the Hut, Ferndown (4 beds), and St. Giles House, the home of Lord Shaftesbury (47 beds). Between them they provided 254 beds and handled over 2,500 cases. Dorset itself looked after 27,111 injured servicemen in V.A.D. hospitals. The nursing staff were all volunteers.

30. Beatrice and Olga Crew with "Fan", deliver-ing bread for King's Bakery, Hinton St. Mary, in 1916, at a time when the 4 lb. loaf cost 8d. As more men joined the forces women replaced them in both factory and field, a major social revolution thus began which led to women get-ting the vote in 1918.

32. (*Bottom right*) A war-time wedding group outside Sherborne Wesleyan church in about 1916.

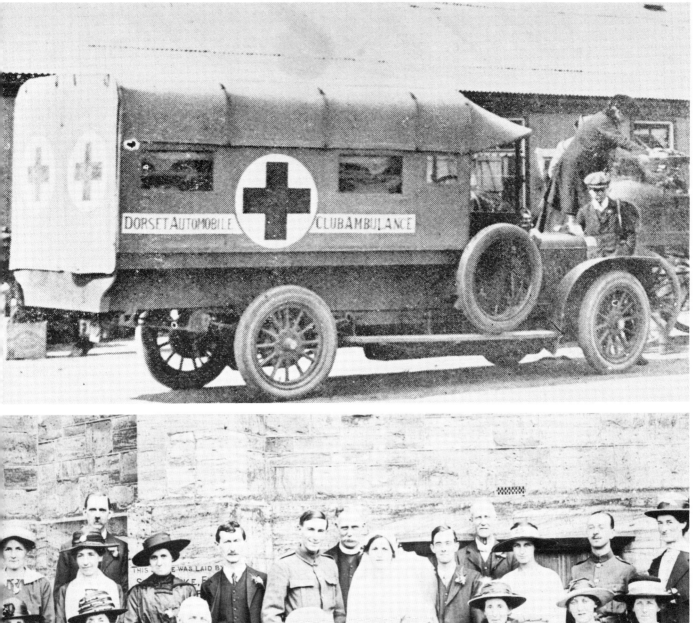

33. Haymaking near Sturminster Newton bridge in 1916. The land was rented by Mr. King, and the men – mostly local tradesmen – were all exempt from military service.

The Years of Peace

1919~1939

34. Gwen Hole at Elm Tree Farm,
Holwell, in 1919.

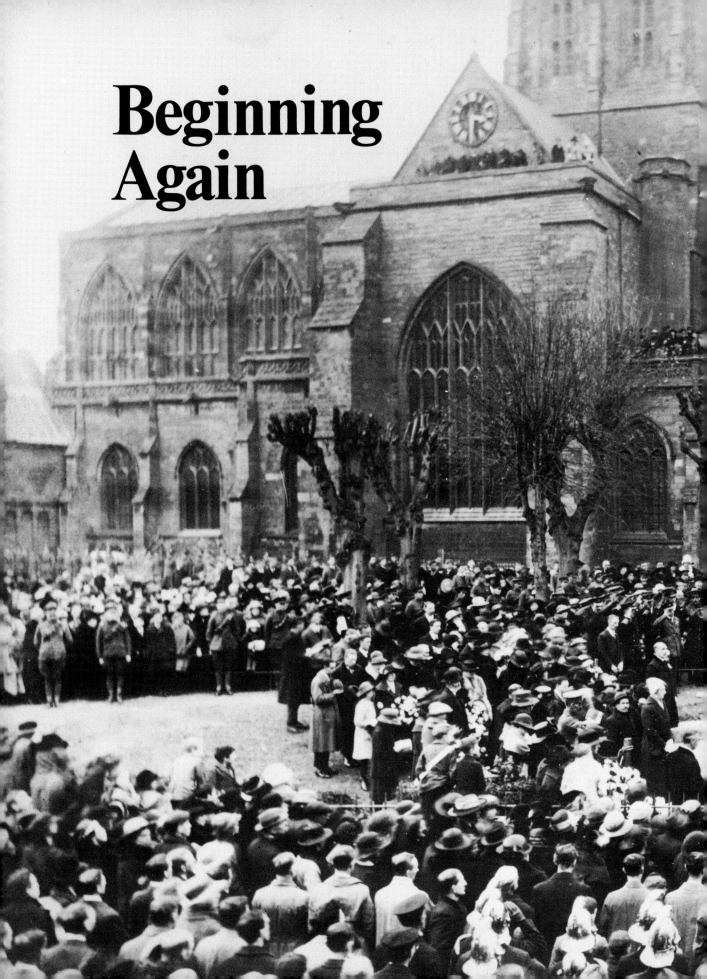

Beginning Again

35. (*Overleaf*) The unveiling of Sherborne War Memorial by the Earl of Shaftesbury and Bishop Josceleyne on Armistice Day, 1921. The 24-foot cross commemorates the 165 Sherbornians killed in the Great War.

36. Swanage beach from beside the Beach Stores & Cafe in 19[...] That summer, the first of peace, a brand new publicity broch[...] proudly announced that: "The beach is divided into three ba[...]ing areas. One is assigned to the ladies, another to the use of men, whilst in the third – proving how up-to-date Swanage h[...] become – mixed bathing is permitted."

37. Inside Weymouth harbour in 1919. The Cosens paddle-steamers were used to ferry out supplies to the ships in Portland Roads throughout the war. Note the steam tugs.

38. Weymouth Esplanade in 1923. In 1925 it was widened to he[...] local unemployment and prevent shingle encroaching on to th[...] famous sands. Each year the rival resorts of Weymouth and Swanage mounted extensive campaigns listing their attraction[...] A 1923 Weymouth brochure remarked on the curve of the Bay[...] "which Lady Eleanor Smith, the clever daughter of Lord Birke[...]head, prefers even to Cannes"; the drinking water, "bright and sparkling of a high degree of purity both chemically and bac-teriologically"; as well as the town's benefits to those sufferi[...] from chest diseases and those "contemplating retirement from a colonial tropical clime."

39. The works outing of the Compton Press, Gillingham, to Weston-super-Mare in 1919. The charabanc was a 20-hp "Garford" belonging to John Stickland, one of Dorset's motor pioneers and amongst the first to open a garage.

40. The unveiling of Dorchester's War Memorial by Lord Ellenborough on 24 May 1921, "at a time when the trivial round, the common task had ended, and, following a day of effulgent sunshine, the sun was sinking slowly in the west." The matter of a memorial to the town's 237 dead had been allowed to lapse, and only pressure by "The Comrades of the Great War" had hurried the Council into action.

▷ 41. Looking down Cheap St., Sherborne, in the mid-1920s Note that the town was still by gas.

Town Life

42. Channon & Sons chain-driven Daimler, possibly in Weymouth in 1919. This Dorchester-based charabanc was used extensively during the war to take injured men on outings from Dorset's V.A.D. Hospitals Note the pneumatic tyres.

43. Poole High St. in about 1920.

44. West St., Bridport in 1930.

45, 46. Two views of Dorchester in 1930. *Top*: Cornhill. *Bottom*: High West St. Perhaps at no other time was Dorset life so perfectly balanced between the old and the new. A "Servants Registry" in South St. still offered to find jobs for scullery maids, kitchen maids, and "tweenies"; but the town had its own somewhat erratic electricity supply, and out in the country roads were being tarmac'ed, houses connected to the telephone, and remote hamlets made accessible to the 20th century.

47. An Italian organ-grinder with his monkey somewhere off Darby's Lane, Poole in the mid-1930s. Immigrant Italians, many of whom sold ice-cream in summer and roast-chestnuts in winter, were a familiar sight between the wars.

48. Gillingham High St. in 1924. Note that "Hot & Cold Lunches" were available at 1s. 6d. Gillingham's growth to 3,200 by that year had been guaranteed by its position on the edge of the Blackmoor Vale and the arrival of the railway. The calf-market, cheese factory, bacon curing, and dairy depot were all by-products of the London rail link.

49. Bridport Carnival in June 1922.

50. Wimborne High St. and Square on a market day in 1923. Out of the eighteen shops on the left-hand side only three still carry on the same trade.

51. Weymouth station in 1931. The centre platforms belonged to the Great Western Railway, and those to left and right to Southern Railway. In 1931 Dorset possessed 72 stations and halts: today there are 20.

52. The "Royal" in Weymouth, 1925. A regular coach outing that took visitors to the Wishing Well at Upwey.

A Changing Dorset

53 (*Overleaf*), 54. County Council road-mending gangs at work near Sturminster Newton (*overleaf*), and Holnest (*top*) in the early 1930s. Continual road widening and tarring made it necessary for the A.A. – who had opened the first roadside filling station in 1922 – to report Dorset road conditions weekly in local papers. Note that in both photographs the humble horse, so quick to be made redundant, was needed to haul the water waggon and tar boiler!

55. Jack Hurst, Geordie Rickards, and Charlie Greening erec[...] telephone posts near "The Plough", Manston, in 1937. The c[...] necting charge was 30s., and the annual rental £4.

6. Archie Garrett, who never learnt to drive, at the wheel of a Model "T" Ford in Thornford, in 1926. After selling a horse for £25 the Garretts, a family of thatchers, bought this their first car second-hand for £50. Even new the Model "T" then cost just over £100.

57. Frank Thorne of Cerne Abbas, once a local carrier, at the wheel of the first daily bus into Dorchester, a 32-hp chain-driven "Albion", in 1919. Trade vehicles were excluded from Duty, but their maximum permitted speed was 12 m.p.h. By 1918 2,450 vehicles were Dorset-registered.

58. Swanage lifeboat, the "Herbert Sturmey", about to start on her last voyage before being replaced by the "Thomas Markby" in 1928. The 37½-foot self-righting "row-an-sail" lifeboat was amongst the last of her type to be taken into service. She had a quiet life, rescuing only four holidaymakers in ten years. Left to right are: Alex Powell, Basil Powell, Frank Inman, Charlie Brown, W. F. T. Powell, Sid Dyke, Harry Bartlett, Bill Dyke (coxswain), Bob Brown.

59. The Duke of York, later King George VI, opening Weymouth bridge in July 1930. The bridge's construction had been delayed since 1914, and when finished it had cost £85,789. The stones of the old bridge were bought by Sir Ernest Debenham to rebuild Briantspuddle bridge. Note the Pathé newsreel film team on the engine-room roof.

60. The scene in Poole Harbour at the opening of the new Hamworthy bridge by Alderman H. S. Carter on 9 March 1927. The old bridge had been privately owned and in order to demolish it the council had first bought it for £16,000.

61. Amongst Dorset's first chain supermarkets was the Parkstone branch of the International Stores, here photographed in the mid-1920s. Bacon and cheese were both 8d. a lb., butter was 5d., and Australian wine 2s. 9d. a bottle.

62. Wimborne Volunteer Fire Brigade with their motorised engine in 1932. The engine, a Merryweather equipped with a Hatfield cylinder pump, was capable of pumping 500 gallons a minute, and of throwing a jet of water over the Minster tower.

63. Pamphill Forge in the early 1920s. As general smithy on the Kingston Lacy estate Frank Bowden (*right*) did much agricultural work for the tenant farmers. He never employed an apprentice, but occasionally hired assistance for night work.

The Countryman

64. "Twisty" Turner making skeps at Thornicombe, near Blandford, in the 1930s. The wheat straw skeps were used taking swarms.

66. Harry Brown, head-keeper the Hambro's Milton Abbey state, tending to the broody bi along Horsepath Ride in th early 1930s. Each hen sat on clutch of eighteen pheasant e and in this way the shoot rea some 11,000 pheasant. Four drives in season over Delcom valley could produce a bag o 1,000 birds a day.

65. Sydling St. Nicholas in 19 The thatcher at work was pro ably George Thomas, and apa from him the small communi then supported two carriers, joiner, carpenter, and black smith.

68. Douglas and Elizabeth Hindley moving the poultry house on their 60-acre Elm Tree Farm, Sturminster Newton, in 1929. The Bullnose Morris cost £18 second-hand, petrol was 1s. 6d. a gallon, and eggs 7d. a dozen.

67. A Fontmell Magna hurdle-maker "beating-up" in Fontmell Wood in about 1937. A good man could make ten hurdles in a day. Of all rural craftsmen the hurdle-maker has proved the most adaptable, and although his work is no longer needed to fold or pen sheep it remains much in demand.

69. West Mills workshop and forge, Dorchester, in 1932. The workshop bonded wheels and did general repair work. Much of the belt-driven machinery would have been powered by a small Blackstone or Lister petrol-engine mounted elsewhere.

70. Harry Chinchen and Walter Brown in an underground wo ing of Purbeck stone in 1930 near Swanage. Note the pillared hard stone supporting the roof in the background. Eric Benfield in a "Purbeck Shop", first published in 1940, remembers what i was like below. "Underground there was a complete freedom from any contact of sound or sight; no one knew I was there – except for the light of one candle there was nothing in my world except blackness. If I dropped it or blew it out there wa the darkness of doom itself everywhere; thunder, lightning, rain of falling stars might all appear on earth, Prime Ministe and the price of beer might fall, but nothing of them all could reach down to where I was."

Commerce

71. Dorchester Unemploymen[t]
Centre in the early 1930s. The
Depression left its mark on
farming and 250,000 farm wo[rk]
ers left the land in search of
employment. The governmen[t]
dropped its guarantee to farm[ers]
for a minimum wage, and whe[at]
that had been 80s. a quarter i[n]
1920 fell to 42s.

72. Left to right: Ann Hatcha[rd],
Eileen Prangnell, and Gertie
Rivers hand-painting tradition[al]
Poole pottery in 1926. Most o[f]
the ware dating from this peri[od]
was designed by Truda Carter[,]
and by 1930 the company wa[s]
employing 30 paintresses to h[elp]
meet the demand.

73. Inside F. J. Barnes's mason['s]
shop at Wide St., Portland, in
1926. In the foreground holdi[ng]
mason's mallets are, left to
right: Jimmy Durston, Tom
Croad, Harry Hawkins. The s[hop]
is now a concrete works.

74. A typical Dorchester shop
front of the 1920s, T. Pouncy['s]
"Saddler & Tobacconist" shop
in Cornhill.

The Coastline

75. (*Overleaf*) The Greek steamer "Preveza" grounded on Chesil in January 1920. The "Preveza" was uninsured, and after taking on coal and stores at Portland sailed for Cardiff where she was refused a cargo. Bound for Rotterdam from Cardiff she ran on to Chesil in thick fog. Once the crew had been rescued local tradesmen with unpaid bills nailed writs to her mast. An attempt to haul the "Preveza" off failed when the towing tug's anchor chain got caught in its own propeller, and had in turn to be held off through a two-day storm; by the end of which the "Preveza" had broken in two.

76. The "Madeleine Tristan" aground near Chesil Cove in September 1930. Bound in ballast for Le Havre the French grain schooner grounded during a south-westerly gale. Her wreckage became a familiar sight, and although a Mr. Cohen bought the hulk for £1 he never did more than cut out her masts and mount them on a converted Lowestoft drifter with which he hoped to salvage iron from other Dorset wrecks.

77. The barquentine "Waterwitch". Built in 1871 at Poole the "Waterwitch" was the last square-rigged sailing ship registered at a British port as carrying cargo. She made her last voyage in 1936.

Poole Quay in 1931.

79. The Cosens & Co. 257-ton, 175-foot, paddle steamer "Consul" in Weymouth Bay in 1938. The Consul" had been built in the 19th century and as the "Duke of Devonshire" was a familiar sight on the Lulworth, Bridport, Seaton, Sidmouth beaches. In 1914 she was renamed H.M.S. "Duke", converted into a minesweeper, and used in the Dardanelles. Between 1939 and 1945 she was employed in Contraband Examination. In 1968, after waiting for a year for a buyer at £9,750, the "Consul" was towed to Southampton and broken-up.

80 Sandbanks in the early 1930s. The development of what had once been a waste land into one of Dorset's most popular beaches was nearly halted in 1934 when the residents of the narrow headland attempted to have a toll-gate installed and the area banned to all but themselves.

82. Sheep shearing by hand at a Studland fa in 1920. By the end of the decade most she. were powered by electricity or a small petr motor.

81. West Bay, Bridport, on August bank-holiday 1930. The rail fare from London was 33s. 6d. 3rd Class.

Farming

83. Mr. Riggs at Roke Far[m],
Bere Regis, in 1927 on a Fo[rd]
son tractor. Dorset farmers
employed 13,000 heavy hor[ses]
between them, and there w[ere]
probably no more than a h[un]
dred tractors in the whol[e]
county.

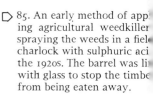

85. An early method of appl[y]
ing agricultural weedkiller[s:]
spraying the weeds in a fiel[d of]
charlock with sulphuric aci[d in]
the 1920s. The barrel was li[ned]
with glass to stop the timbe[r]
from being eaten away.

84. A gyro-tiller, or rotary
plough, being pulled behind [a]
"crawler" to break up heavy
ground in the mid-1930s.

86. Turning the hay at Thorn[hill]
Farm, Marnhull, in 1925. The
Blackstone's combined swath
turner, collector, and side del[iv]
ery rake was then amongst t[he]
most modern of horse-drawn
implements.

88. Dorset smallholders, the Moore family, gathering in the hay under Shillingstone Hill in 1925.

89. Beatrice Hole at Elm Tree Farm, Holwell, in 1919.

87. The receiving platform of the Sturminster
Newton & District Farmers in the early 1920s.
This early co-operative was formed in 1913
when farmers had to find their own outlets, and
taken over by the Milk Marketing Board in 1937.
Much of the milk was turned into cheese and
sent by rail to London. The man in the cart,
Mr. King, for a time delivered Sturminster Newton's milk on foot, carrying yoked churns on a
twice-daily three-hour round when milk was
three-farthings a pint.

90. Picking water-cress at Lawrence's farm near
Shaftesbury in the late 1920s.

91. Sheep being dipped near Shillingstone in the 1920s. Note that the men are all wearing gaiters. Although the sheep dip was originally used to prevent sheep scab it has been more recently employed to kill the eggs of the sheep maggot fly.

92. A general view of a sheep sale in progress at Dorchester Market in 1935. A registered Dorset Horn ewe fetched up to 80s and a Dorset Down 70s.

93. (*Overleaf*) The "Wolsey Bell" being returned to Sherborne in 1934 after being hauled into town by 70 boys from Sherborne School. The bells, a gift from Cardinal Wolsey, were the heaviest peal of eight in the country, and the 2½-ton Tenor Bell had been recast at the Whitechapel Foundry at a cost of £140.

94. Burning 2,000 carcasses at Sturminster Newton in April 19 following the discovery of two foot-and-mouth infected calv on a Market Day. This, Dorset's most serious outbreak of the disease between the wars, led to the Ministry of Agriculture prohibiting the movement of all the livestock at the mark After employing local labour to dig trenches, and buying 60 tons of coal, 778 pigs, 326 sheep, 679 calves, and 217 other cat had to be slaughtered and burnt.

95. Collecting water from the milkman during the 1927 drought, in Iwerne Minster.

96. Lloyd George outside Tolpuddle Methodist Chapel in 1937, the year the chapel was restored.

97. The T.U.C. procession, led by the banner of the National Union of Agricultural Workers, returning down High West St., Dorchester, from Maumbury Ring on 2 September 1934, after celebrating the opening of the T.U.C. Memorial Cottages at Tolpuddle by Andrew Conley, President of the T.U.C., three days earlier. 1934 marked the centenary of the Martyrs' trial and deportation.

98, 99. Two views of the Maiden Castle Excavations of 1934 to 1937. *Top*: A general view of the southern portal. *Bottom*: Cutting through the innermost western rampart. The dig was sponsored by the Society of Antiquaries, and supported by the Duchy of Cornwall – who owned the site – the Dorset Natural History & Archaeological Society, and the Office of Works; was directed by Dr. Mortimer Wheeler, with the aid of his wife Tessa Verney-Wheeler, and Lieut.-Colonel C. D. Drew. The dig, thanks perhaps to the size of the site and the extent of the finds, was much publicised and did a great deal both for Dorset and archaeology. A hundred assistants helped each year on the site, and the general public were encouraged to visit it for themselves. 64,000 2d. postcards were sold in this way, and although the entire four-year excavation cost only £5,363, much of this money came from donations and various forms of fund-raising.

100. T. E. Lawrence outside Hut F12 at Bovington Camp in 1924. Lawrence had joined the Tank Corps under the name of Shaw the previous year, and worked in the Quartermaster's Stores until his transfer to the R.A.F. in 1926. Whilst at Bovington Lawrence bought "Cloud's Hill", the Moreton cottage he was to return to whenever possible and where he was living at the time of his fatal motorbike accident in 1935. It was at "Cloud's Hill" that he condensed "Seven Pillars of Wisdom" for its 1926 publication, and the isolated cottage came to symbolise Lawrence's need to escape from the mythology of being Colonel "Lawrence of Arabia". Of "Cloud's Hill" he once wrote: ". . . the cottage is alone in a dip in the moor, very quiet, very lonely, very bare. A mile from camp. Furnished with a bed, a bicycle, three chairs, 100 books, a gramophone of parts, a table. Many windows, oak trees, an ilex, birch, firs, rhododendron, laurels, heather. Dorsetshire to look at."

101. Thomas Hardy outside Portland lighthouse with Marie Stopes – who then lived in it, on the day after the Prince of Wales' visit to Max Gate in 1923. Both Hardy and Dr. Stopes were at the height of their fame, Hardy as the "veteran of Wessex", the nation's best-loved and best-known writer, and Marie Stopes for her outspoken views on Birth Control. If Hardy's work sums up the vanishing rural England of the 19th century, that of Marie Stopes belongs totally to the 20th. In 1921 she had set up in London's East End the world's first Birth Control Clinic and was attacked by both clergy and moralists. But her book "Wise Parenthood" sold half a million copies in the six months following its publication. Hardy died in 1928 and is buried in Stinsford. Marie Stopes lived on until 1958.

102. The Prince of Wales, l
Edward VIII and the Duke
Windsor, flanked by his en
age and the Mayor, Lore
King, greeting officials at T
O' the Town on his visit to
chester in 1923. After lunch
with Thomas Hardy at M
Gate the Prince went on
Maiden Castle, Upwey, ar
Weymouth.

103. The "Dance of the Plo
being performed at Dorche
in 1938 by the Iwerne Mins
Folk Dancers. Other traditio
Dorset dances are "Bricks &
Mortar", "Dance of the Bro
stick", "Heel & Toe", and th
"Ring Dance."

104. The fire at Lulworth Castle
on 29 August 1929 which left it
completely gutted. The fire
broke out on the top floor, and
firemen from Dorchester, Swanage, Weymouth, and Poole almost had it under control when
the water supply ran out.

105. The owner of Lulworth
Castle, Mr. Herbert Weld, sits
helplessly on the lawn amid
salvaged furniture and watches
the destruction of his family
home. Most of the paintings and
furniture were saved by teams
of servants, estate workers, firemen and soldiers.

106. Princess Margaret shaking hands with Admiral Sir Dudley North, captain of the Royal Yacht "Victoria & Albert", before leaving Weymouth after the Royal Family's visit of July 1939. Princess Elizabeth is hidden behind her mother. It was the first time the entire Royal Family had visited the town for 150 years.

107. Boys of the "Hitler Jugend", the Nazi Youth Movement, visiting the County Hospital, Dorchester, in 1936. The German party was entertained by Toc H, the Y.M.C.A., and at a Royal luncheon. That same week the *County Chronicle* announced that an Air Raid Precaution Service was to be set up by the Government.

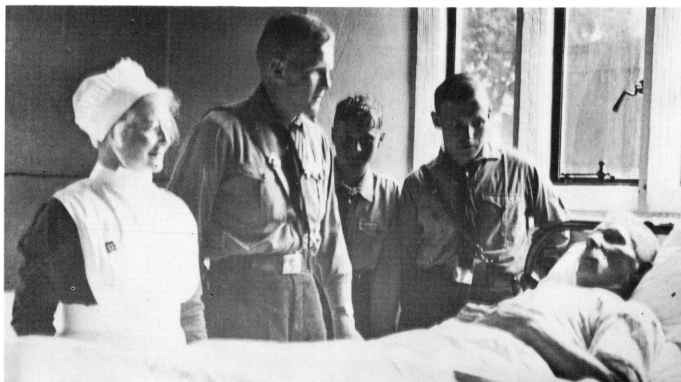

The People's War

1939~1945

108. The Civil Defence and Home Guard cleaning up in Sherborne after the raid of 30 September 1940 in which 18 people were killed, 32 injured, 776 properties damaged, and 300 bombs dropped in the space of a few minutes. The raid began when 150 bombers were turned away from Yeovil Junction by fighters, and jettisoned their bombs over Sherborne in what was almost a straight line. Clearing up the debris was made difficult by an unexploded bomb in Cheap St., and fractured mains service pipes. The W.V.S. organised communal feeding, and a £2,200 Relief Fund was set up.

The Threat of Invasion

109. (*Overleaf*) Bridport's aluminium scrap-heap in 1940. Lord Beaverbrook's appeal for scrap to offset Spitfire and Hurricane losses in the Battle of Britain led to park railings, bedsteads and bicycles finding their way on to the local heap. The heap of pots and pans was of no immediate practical value but was an important method of involving the housewife in the fight against the Luftwaffe.

110. Messrs. Wyatt, Wills, and Cook cleaning American rifles supplied to the Home Guard a part of Lease Lend, at Symond bury in 1940. The rifles had be stored in grease since 1918, an were cleaned by pouring boili water over them.

1. "Fougasse", or inshore oil defences by which the sea was set alight, being demonstrated off ⌐dland in 1940. The demonstration was something of a disaster in that the wind changed, the ⌐ffs caught alight, and the senior officers who had come to view this anti-invasion exercise ⌐re forced to beat a hasty retreat from their observation platform.

112. Winston Churchill with General Brooks, inspecting a 9.2-inch Howitzer emplacement of Southern Command at Parkstone, shortly after becoming Prime Minister in May 1940.

113. Part of the 133 ships of the Reserve Fleet lined up in Weymouth Bay for inspection by George VI on 12 August 1939, three weeks before the declaration of war. The Fleet was commanded by Vice-Admiral Sir Max Horton, and composed mostly of officers and men of the R.N.R. and the R.N.V.R. Amongst the ships in the fleet was the aircraft carrier "Courageous", sunk by a "U-boat" within six weeks; and the battleships "Ramillies", used in the D-Day bombardment of Normandy, and "Iron Duke", Jellicoe's flagship at the Battle of Jutland in 1916.

114. Collecting the milk at Shroton in 1941.

115. Arthur Stickley in Hall & Woodhouse's two-horse dray, and Bobby Roper in the single horse, outside "The New Inn" – now "The Stour Inn", Blandford in 1941. If Dorset milk was urgently needed to meet the demand of children evacuated into the area, locally-brewed beer was never more popular. "Beer makes for the British cheerfulness which is undefeatable. So stick to beer", stated a war-time advertisement.

6. Fred & Billy Lee, late of London's Elephant & Castle, at Springfield House, Gillingham,
fter being evacuated in 1939. Householders were initially paid 8s. 6d. a week for each child
illeted with them, and once the novelty had worn off evacuation led to endless problems
etween the "heathenish" rural "yokels", and the "loutish, verminous, bed-wetting" urban ur-
ins that had been forced upon them.

117. Members of Weymouth's war-time St. John Ambulance Brigade alongside "Khaki", an ambulance presented to them by the American Red Cross in 1940. Left to right: Pte. Bennett, Miss L. Barley, Mrs. Groves (Commandant, Red Cross), Mrs. Bartlett (Lady Superintendent, S.J.A.B.), L/Cpl. Haines.

118. A German "Dornier 215" shot down in a field of kale near Fleet, Chickerell, in the summer of 1940. The plane was surprised by fighters from Warmwell whilst attacking shipping in West Bay. On being captured the pilot offered round "Players" cigarettes looted from a N.A.A.F.I. in newly occupied France.

⌂ 119. Clearing up in Newstead Rd., Weymouth, after the raid of 11 August 1940, in which three houses were demolished and the remainder of the terrace damaged. The area's first raid took place over Portland in July, and from then on most of Weymouth and Portland's 51 raids took place on either a Thursday or Sunday. Weymouth's last raid took place on 28 May 1944, a week prior to D-Day, and by then 83 people had been killed and 7,417 properties damaged. Swanage and Poole were also bombed, but Weymouth and Portland were amongst the hardest hit of all coastal front-line towns.

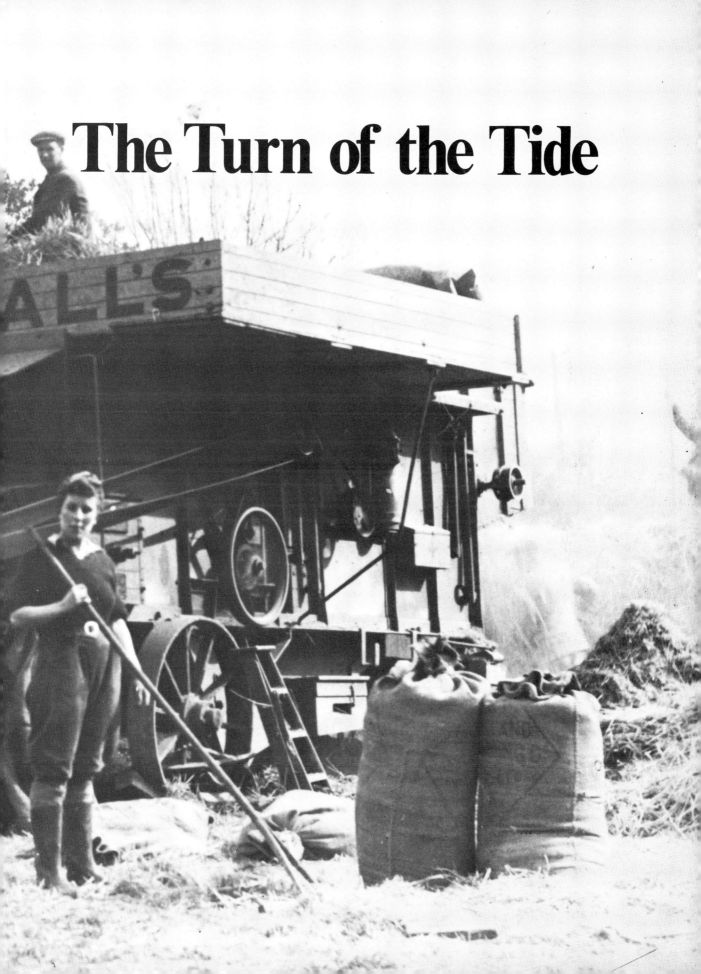

The Turn of the Tide

120. (*Overleaf*) Marshall's threshing tackle being used at Arthur Field's Shillingstone farm in 1942. The Land Girls either lived on the farm or in local hostels where they could be hired for special duties.

121. A Bomb Disposal team led by Lieutenant Woods, Bomb Disposal Officer for Dorset, relaxing after hauling up a 1,000-kilo unexploded bomb from 28 feet beneath Melcombe Avenue, Weymouth, in June 1944. The bomb had fallen during the raid of 28 May, in which Weymouth Hospital was badly damaged, and it took the Bomb Disposal team five days to get it to the surface.

122. A Civil Defence Decontamination Squad on exercise in North Square, Dorchester, 1941. It was thought that coastal areas would be subject to gas attack when the wind was in the right direction. Between 1940 and 1944 629 high explosives, 6,150 incendiaries, 30 oil bombs, and 5 parachute mines fell on Dorchester. The town suffered one casualty.

DANGER GAS

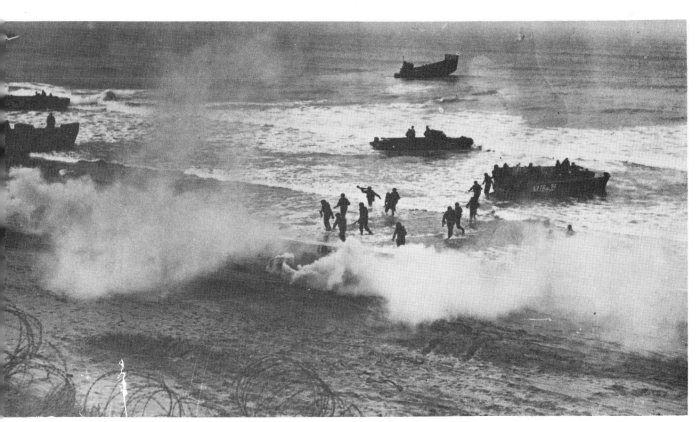

123. Commandos in training for the Bruneval raid, near Weymouth in early 1942. The raid on a German radar post on the French coast on 27 February 1942 was completely successful. The commandos were taken off by the Navy after attacking, dismantling, and removing most of the equipment mounted in the post.

124. "German" prisoners are led away at the end of Operation "Demon", a joint A.R.P. and Home Guard Exercise held in Sherborne in May 1943. The building in the background is the ruined Foster's Newland Rd. Infant School, destroyed during the 1940 raid on the town.

125. A B.O.A.C. Boeing flying boat coming in to land in Poole harbour in 1943. The Boeings were used on the African supply route, and after crossing the Atlantic to be serviced at Boeing's Baltimore works returned to Poole via the Azores carrying V.I.P. passengers. Poole Harbour Yacht Club was requisitioned as a Marine Terminal. Amongst those who used the service were Mountbatten, Slim, Wavell, and Sikorsky.

126. Pupils of Wimborne St. Giles All Age School Young Farmers Club extracting and weighing the honey from their hives in 1944. The Club was founded in the 1930s by Clarence Quelch as Nectar Ltd., as a means by which children could learn something of farming and finance. During the war the Club's activities expanded to include rural crafts, pigs, rabbits, sheep, and an energetic "Dig for Victory" campaign. The Club farmed four acres of glebe land and was only dissolved on Mr. Quelch's retirement in 1962.

127. Wimborne's Auxiliary Fire Service leading the parade through the town during "Warships Savings Week" in 1941. The Wimborne Fire Service went as far afield as Southampton, Plymouth, and Bristol to help during heavy bombing raids.

D~Day to Victory

128. (*Overleaf*) American troops
aboard landing-craft in Portland
harbour only hours before taking part in the D-Day landings
on 6 June 1944. In 1943 it had
been decided to make Dorset a
major training and staging area
for the invasion of Europe, and
in November Dorchester Barracks were handed over to the
Americans. Soon the County
filled with G.I.s, bringing with
them "Hershey Bars" and re-
ports in the newspapers remark-
ing that, "Whilst M.P.s in jeeps
were sure of a swelling roar of
boos and catcalls; pretty girls,
girls on cycles, girls in trousers,
all called forth appreciative re-
marks and whistles". The Dorset coast, to a depth of ten miles,
was made a restricted area. The
beaches at Studland and Ring-
stead, because of their similarity
to the French coast, were used
for pre-invasion training. On D-
Day itself some 34,000 Americans sailed from Dorset ports.

129. Black American troops load-
ing "C" and "K" rations on to
Assault Landing Craft moored
alongside Weymouth Pavilion,
in early June 1944.

30. An American G.I. doing the "Lambeth
Walk" on Weymouth Esplanade prior to boarding a landing craft and sailing for the Normandy
beaches. In the week that led up to the depar-
ture of the Invasion Fleet the lanes and roads
of Dorset were crammed with tanks, trucks,
and troops moving from the main inland com-
pounds to the embarkation ports of Poole,
Weymouth, and Portland.

32. American Rangers on Burton Bradstock
beach in April 1944 rehearsing their D-Day
attack on the German guns at Pointe du Hoc.
Either side of the cliff ladder can be seen grapnel
ladders fired from rockets mounted on landing
craft. The German guns controlled both "Utah"
and "Omaha" beaches, and although the 2nd
and 5th Ranger Battalions met with stiff oppo-
sition they succeeded in their climb; only to
find that the guns had been moved.

31. Crack American troops of the 1st Division,
veterans of N. Africa and Italy, being packed
into landing craft in Weymouth harbour before
sailing for France on D-Day. 4,000 ships and
130,000 men – amongst them the 1st Battalion
the Dorsetshire Regiment who landed on "Gold"
beach as part of the 50th Division – took part in
the invasion. The two-day journey in small boats
was a nightmare. The flat-bottomed landing
craft rolled badly, and for most people the voyage was a mixture of seasickness, hunger,
cramp, tiredness, and nerves. The 1st Division
landed on "Omaha" beach at dawn and suffered
the highest invasion casualties.

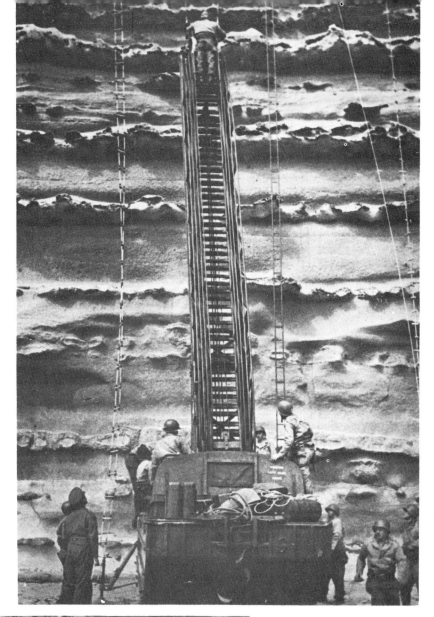

133. American landing craft
gathered in Portland harbour
after the Normandy landings.
Some were specially adapted for
cooking, as medical units, or for
repair work; and once the initial
landings had taken place were
used to ferry men and supplies
out to the troopships. Between
6 June 1944 (D-Day) and 8 May
1945 (V.E. Day) 517,816 men and
144,093 vehicles embarked at
either Portland or Weymouth
before sailing to France.

134. The Stand Down Parade of the 2nd (Dorset) Battalion of the Home Guard on the football field behind the Marabout Barracks, Dorchester, in December 1944. Lieutenant-Colonel Drew and General Sir Henry Jackson took the salute, and Canons Bowess (Dorchester), Daniell (Litton Cheney), and. Helps (Puddletown) led the prayers. At its height the Battalion strength rose to 1,900 men.

135. The first "U-boat" to reach a British port after Germany's unconditional surrender on 8 May 1945 was "U 249", here seen entering Portland harbour under the armed escort of a trawler and sloop on 10 May. The issue of Admiralty orders to "U-boat" captains asking them to surface and await capture led to submarines appearing within ∼ few miles of the Dorset coast. "U 249" had a crew of 5 officers and 47 ratings.